More...
Dribble Drabble
Process – Oriented Art

By
Deya Brashears
with
Lea Brashears

Illustrations by Georgianne Gaines Meeker

Published by Circle Time Publishing - Orinda, California

Acknowledgements

Dedicated to our dear cousin, Joellen Blanchard who was Deya's playmate and to our cousin, Nevea Kohout who was our artistic mentor.

Acknowledgments are made to Christopher Curtis for the cover illustration.

We want to especially thank the students at Chabot College, Santa Rosa Junior College, and Diablo Valley College for sharing their ideas and creativity. Without them, this book would not be possible.

We claim no originality for these art experiences. They were developed through experimentation and as contributions from Deya's many students.

Technical Assistance by
DMC Publications
2113 Creekwood Drive
Fort Collins, Colorado 80525

Workshop Information
Deya Brashears
1 Corte Del Rey
Orinda, California 94563
(510) 376-3516

Distributed by
Gryphon House, Inc.
P.O. Box 217
Mt. Rainier, Maryland 20822

Introduction

The first collection of art experiences is published in Deya's book, *Dribble Drabble*, c. 1985, and it is because of the success of this publication that we continued to create and collect more art experiences, thus enabling us to present this second art collection, *More Dribble Drabble*. The format of *More Dribble Drabble* is the same as in *Dribble Drabble* and we hope that you will find it just as easy to use and just as much fun to explore.

The collections in both publications focus on process-oriented, hands-on expressions in art. The emphasis is on the **process** rather than the finished **product** and can easily be adapted for infant and toddlers as well as school age curricula. All of these activities are quickly and easily set-up and provide lots of fun for all ages - yes, even us old kids.

Table of Contents

Creating a Stimulating Art Environment

Teachers and parents often ask me what they should provide for their children to give them a quality art experience. There are four basic areas that should be a part of every art environment: easels, a free art table, tactile or sensory experience, and an activity center. The children should be able to choose from at least two of these areas each day, and in an ideal setting, all four areas can be used. The following are the items I recommend to ensure high quality of the art environment; they are in priority order. Let's take a look at each area in detail and discuss its artistic value.

Easels

The easel is the one art experience that many teachers and parents would prefer to do without; easels take up space, and mixing and cleaning paints can get routine. However, there is incredible value from this form of expression that cannot be derived from any other form of art. A child develops from the head down and from the trunk out; therefore, the last things to develop physically are the fine muscles in the fingers and toes. Easels provide the perfect vertical experience to aid this development. Children all over the world from the beginning of time have drawn on the walls--much to the dismay of their parents--which tells us that the natural means of artistic expression throughout life is in the vertical plane. This is available with the easel. If a child cannot yet hold a pencil or pen, he or she may not have any means of written artistic expression unless an easel is available to him. It is vital that we take the time to provide quality easel expression.

Some easel suggestions:

» Purchasing an expensive easel is not necessary: tape paper to a wall or door or use the sliding glass door or a smooth fence outside.

» If you buy easels, consider getting some that attach to the wall to conserve floor space. Centers should have at least two vertical surfaces for every ten children.

» Don't use only rectangular paper. Cut the paper into other shapes and forms or cut shapes from the paper and create negative space. Children like shapes, such as flags, hearts, circles, animals, and others.

» Use good quality easel paper rather than computer paper or thin newsprint.

» Use good quality paint; clear, bright colors should be used.

» Paint brushes don't have to be brushes--try using feathers, cotton swabs, sponges, flowers, pine branches, green onions, gadgets, or whatever seems interesting to you.

» Add salt or glitter to the paint for a different effect. Don't always use paint--try chalk. Tape four different colors of chalk together with masking tape; when the child draws on the paper, many different colors will emerge. Put some liquid starch, buttermilk, or sweetened condensed milk at the easel with the chalk. The child can compare and observe the effects using each.

» Offer this experience both indoors and outside.

Role of the Teacher in the Easel Area

The teacher must make sure each day that the paints are mixed well and that the paint tubs are full. Brushes should be in good condition and there should be some short- and some long-handled brushes. Good quality easel paper should be plentiful and easily available. The teacher should ask permission to put the artist's name on the artwork. Ask the child where his or her name should go. This shows respect for the child and his or her work. When the artwork is finished, the child should hang it to dry--the teacher may need to help with this. New paper should then be placed on the easel for the next child to use. During the actual process, the teacher may want to encourage language development by asking the child, "Would you like to tell me about your picture?" Sometimes the child will have a long story and sometimes he or she will not want to say anything, which is fine, too. It is, of course, inappropriate to ask the child what the picture is or say, "Is that a bird?" This kind of question can intimidate the child into feeling that it "should" look like something, when the picture most likely is not anything more than colors and designs . Easels and the easel experience should always be inviting.

Free Art Table

This should be an area that requires very little supervision by an adult. Art supplies can be set out for the children to use at will. The table should have these supplies:

- » felt pens
- » crayons
- » pencils
- » envelopes
- » scissors
- » stamps
- » sticky dots
- » hole punches
- » various sizes, shapes, and colors of paper
- » cellophane or clear tape (with a bottom-weighted tape dispenser)
- » staplers (good, heavy quality staplers that work and have plenty of staples)
- » other tools that might lend themselves to creative expression

Good tools and appropriate supervision will eliminate accidents. This table should be totally free of any models or "color-in" types of activities. You will be amazed by what the children create with unrestricted options.

Role of the Teacher at the Free Art Table

In this area, the teacher mainly keeps supplies furnished, makes sure the child's name is on the artwork, and tidies the table occasionally. (Children love to make a mess but they do not like to sit down to one.) Keep supplies plentiful, in good working order, and attractive. Put the supplies on the table each day. Many schools feel that open shelves mean that children can help themselves to supplies at will; however, I have seen much more involvement when the supplies are out and on the table, enticing them to create.

Tactile or Sensory Area

No one of any age tires of tactile expression, and this kind of experience should be available to the children as often as possible. I like to use clean kitty litter pans because they offer a flat bottom and ample size for such items. Some items that work well with children are sand, mud, corn meal, rice, beans, warm water, alfalfa, potpourri, "goop" (cornstarch and water), hay, macaroni, coffee grounds (dried), bird seed, or again, whatever you feel offers a great sensory experience. We tend to forget about good old water play, and this is still one of the most soothing experiences we can provide. Occasionally, you can color the water and add some bubbles. Sponges, pumps, hoses, and various containers also add to the fun. Sand (indoors, rather than just in the sandbox) and good old-fashioned mud also provide lots of options. Coffee grounds can be placed in a microwave or a regular oven for a few minutes to dry out. These grounds smell wonderful and feel like course sand. Other options include modeling materials such as clay, play dough, sand clay, and others. Sensory or tactile experiences are ageless and nearly irresistible.

Role of the Teacher in the Tactile or Sensory Area

The teacher should try the sensory experience, especially if it involves modeling mediums. Is the clay too hard or too dry? Is the water too cold? Are the beans beginning to have an odor? Occasionally, the teacher sweeps or mops the area to keep it safe and inviting.

Activity Center

This area definitely depends on the adult to make it work. The adult, of course, does not do the work for the children nor does he or she make a model to copy; however, adults are necessary to ensure activity flow and supervise the children. Supplies must be replenished, and some common guidelines should be offered, although variations discovered by the children are encouraged at all times. There is no "right way" to do these activities. The various activities offered in *More Dribble Drabble* and in *Dribble Drabble* would fall into this category; I would place them on the activity table.

Role of the Teacher in the Activity Center

This area, as I have said, requires adult interaction. It is most successful when the adult sits down with the child(ren) and chats informally. The teacher may want to do some of the activities, too, but BE CAREFUL NOT TO MAKE A MODEL for the child to copy or aspire to. Keep it open and simple; put names on the activities; and keep the table tidy and inviting.

Final Thoughts

To sum up: If you have a minimal staff, offering the easel and the free art area will provide a creative, fun, and exciting experience for all children. The other two areas--sensory or tactile and activity--should also be offered, but they are not always possible each day. Remember:

» Vary your choices and move things around.

» Offer all four art areas both inside and outside.

» Types of paper and colors of paper should be changed to attract children.

» Background music and prints of fine art inspire young artists.

My experience is that when the teacher sits down with the child or children to experience art, the child is much more likely to become more involved and for longer periods. In no way am I advocating "doing" or "modeling" for the children; however, simply sitting down at their level offers your companionship and support. It makes the child feel special. I am careful not to model or produce advanced work, because many enlightening conversations have evolved while I enjoyed the art experience with children. Have fun and they will, too.

A Word About Cost

Most children's centers have limited and tight budgets to work with and directors and teachers are always looking for ways to save money. My experience tells me that in some areas of the art environment there are ways to conserve but in other areas good, quality materials are a must. Let me explain what I mean. In the center where I was a director for 14 years, I saved a great deal of money on paper supplies. Instead of using construction paper or tagboard (both of which are very expensive) I got matte board free from framing shops. The frame shop people were delighted that we wanted it so they would not have to throw it away. One side is colored and the other side is white; I let the child decide which side to use. These scraps would often come in various shapes and sizes and sometimes I would have to cut them into appropriate sizes for the planned activity. I used matte board for almost everything at the activity table--collage, painting, crayons, chalk, sculpture, and others.

I also got other kinds of paper supplies donated. For example, banks gave me envelopes and deposit slips (the kids had a ball with those). Pharmacies gave me tablets of paper that came with various medications and these were often unusual shapes and colors, which the children enjoyed. Printing shops and newspaper companies would give me the ends of the rolls of paper, and computer companies would supply computer paper for drawing. Some greeting card stores would save envelopes for me after holidays--they had to send the cards back to the company but threw away the bright, cheerfully colored envelopes.

While I saved lots of money on those paper supplies, I found that certain areas within the art environment demanded more expensive tools. Children do not use the easel nearly as much when computer paper or newsprint is used as they do when nice white easel paper is available. Paints should be bright and attractive, rather than muted and dull. Good quality staplers, scissors, and tape dispensers are also a must. Crayons and felt pens should be of good quality and should be replaced often--pens that are running out of ink are difficult and frustrating to use.

Using real clay rather than plasticine clay provides a much more pliable and creative clay experience for children. Fresh play dough and "goop" (cornstarch and water) will keep children occupied for hours, but dried out play dough and "goop" will disinterest them immediately. Good white glue is necessary so that children do not get frustrated with the "gluing" experience. Paste and glue provide very different experiences. These may offer variety for the children; however, paste can be somewhat frustrating for young children.

A quality art environment demands quality materials that work well. It takes time, patience, and energy to scrounge around to find appropriate supplies, and it takes price comparing to get the best quality for your budget. The children truly will have a positive art experience if you take the time and make their experience the top priority.

A Word About Food and Art

In some school or center settings, using food as an art medium is not appropriate. Food may not be plentiful, and you may want to impart a philosophical respect for food and those in need. This philosophy is certainly valid, and I encourage you to adhere to it if it is appropriate for you. All of the art experiences that use food as art supplies can easily substitute nonfood products. This is a very personal decision that you and your staff will have to discuss and agree on. We in the profession acknowledge and respect all points regarding this sometimes sensitive issue.

by Deya Brashears

Supplies Needed to Get Started

Here is a list of supplies that you might want to collect for your art environment. This is not a complete list, however it is a good start.

Alcohol
Aluminum foil
Aprons
Balls (small and medium sized)
Balloons
Bangles
Berry baskets
Bleach (liquid)
Bowls (various sizes)
Bows
Boxes (all sizes and shapes)
Brayers (small rollers)
Butcher paper
Buttons
Candles (all colors)
Cellophane
Cellophane tape
Cellophane tape dispenser
Chalk (colored and white)
Cheese graters
Collage items
Combs
Confetti
Construction paper (all colors)
Contact paper (clear)
Cookie cutters
Cookie sheets
Corks
Cornmeal
Cornstarch
Cotton balls
Cotton swabs
Craft sticks
Crayons
Detergent (powdered and liquid)
Double boiler
Driftwood
Dry towels (cloth and paper)
Egg cartons
Electric mixer
Epsom salts
Eye droppers

Fabric pieces
Feathers
Felt pens
Flour
Flower petals (dried)
Food coloring
Funnels (small and large)
Glitter
Glue
Glue brushes
Grass (dried)
Griddle
Hair spray
Hole punches
Hot plate
Ice cube tray
Iron
Knives
Lace
Leaves
Lids
Liquid starch
Liquid tempera
Marbles
Masking tape
Matte board
Measuring cups/spoons
Muffin tins
Needles
Newspaper
Nuts/bolts
Oil
Oven
Paint (all kinds)
Paint brushes
Paper (all kinds)
Pencil sharpener
Pencils (colored)
Pie tins
Pinking shears
Pitchers
Pizza cutter

Plastic bags (sandwich size)
Plaster of Paris
Popsicle sticks
Pot holders
Potato mashers
Potato scrapers
Powdered tempera
Prayons (oiled chalk)
Rags
Ribbons
Rock salt
Rocks
Rubber bands
Rubber cement
Rubber gloves
Salad spinner
Salt
Salt shakers
Sand
Sand sifters
Sandpaper
Sawdust
Scissors
Shaving cream
Sheets of glass
Shells
Soap

Sponges
Spoons
Spray bottles
Stamp pads
Stamps
Stencils
Straws
Strings
Styrofoam (all sizes)
Tempera (liquid and powdered)
Tissue paper
Toilet tissue tubes
Tongs
Toothpicks
Towels
Trays
Twist ties
Velvet
Vinegar
Warming tray
Water colors
Waxed paper
White paper
Wire mesh screening
Wood
Wrapping paper
Yarn

Stages of Art Development

All children pass through a sequential pattern of artistic development. Some go through the various stages quickly; others spend a particularly long time in one stage; and all go back and repeat earlier stages as they progress through this development.

There are three basic stages of children's art: the scribble stage, the basic form stage, and the drawing stage. These three stages can be further divided for better identification.

Let's take a look at the generally accepted stages of art development. Keep in mind that the indicated ages are simply generalizations and not a rigid guide for all children. Also notice that the ages overlap.

Stage 1:   **Scribble Stage.** Ages 2-3--These scribbles involve vertical, horizontal, diagonal, curving, and circular lines. All art is based on scribbles.

Stage 2:   **Vague Shapes.** Ages 2-4--Circles, crosses, squares, rectangles, and other basic shapes are roughly visible. This child does not yet have the motor ability to master the shape.

Stage 3:   **Actual Shapes.** Ages 3-5--This is a single outline of a shape. Motor control is now more refined.

Stage 4:   **Combined Shapes.** Ages 3-5--These are designs created by combining and repeating various shapes. Shapes within shapes are common.

Stage 5:   **Mandalas and Suns.** Ages 3-5--These are so common in children's art that they can be traced to prehistoric times. The mandalas and suns display perfect balance. This is a turning point in children's art because from this stage, we begin to see the emergence of recognizable art.

Stage 6:   **People.** Ages 4-5--These first appear as a large head with the arms and legs extending from the head. Later a trunk and more details appear.

Stage 7:   **Beginning Recognizable Art.** Ages 4-6--These pictures are now identifiable. You may see several unrelated objects on a page. These pictures are built using the figures and shapes mastered during previous stages.

Stage 8   **Later Recognizable Art.** Ages 5-7--The entire page tells a story. You may see birds, trees, people, flowers, suns, houses, and kites. This child may still prefer to draw abstract art; however, this is done with good control and intent.

Glossary of Art Terms

Brayer A small roller, usually made of rubber. Found in art supply stores.

Butcher paper Large white paper that comes on a roll and can be cut or torn off at the size you desire.

Craft sticks Sticks from frozen juice or ice cream bars, or tongue depressors.

Driftwood Oddly shaped wood found at the beach.

Eye dropper Used for medicinal purposes and can be bought at pharmacies.

Liquid starch Blue starch in liquid form found at grocery stores.

Liquid tempera Premixed water-based paint. Found in teacher and art supply stores.

Matte board The material used to frame pictures. One side is a color and the other side is white. Found in frame stores.

Pinking shears Scissors that have a ragged edge to them, thus producing a zig-zag cut. Found in fabric stores.

Powdered tempera The dry form of water-based paint. Found in teacher and art supply stores.

Prayons Chalk that has some oil in it. Found in art supply stores.

Spackling powder This is similar to plaster of Paris, but it sets-up more slowly--about 40 minutes. Found in paint and hardware stores.

Water colors Paints with a high water content. Found in art or teacher supply stores.

Icons

At the top of each activity page you will see an icon. These icons indicate the season or seasons in which this activity would work best. For example, if you saw the all-season and winter icons displayed, you would know that this activity works well any time of year, but especially in winter.

You will also see the minimum age indicated at the top of each activity. For example, 2+ would mean that a two-year-old child--and any age above that--would be able to do that particular activity.

These are merely suggestions--feel free to try them in different seasons or with different age groups.

The icons are displayed below with the appropriate indication.

Winter

Spring

Summer

Fall

All Seasons

Painting

Feet Painting and Prints

Materials Needed:

Large sheet of paper
Paint brush
2 or 3 colors of tempera paint
Soapy water
Towels

Procedure:

1. Place the large sheet of paper on the ground.

2. Have child sit in a chair while you paint the bottom of his or her feet (tickle-tickle.)

3. Allow child to walk on the paper, or to make designs with his or her toes.

4. Child can sit and soak feet in soapy water to get clean and wipe with towels.

Note: Best with warm water and best done outside.

Egg Roll Painting

Materials Needed:

Dish pan
Paper to fit pan
Liquid tempera
Hard boiled egg(s)

Procedure:

1. Place paper in bottom of pan.

2. Squirt a little paint onto paper.

3. Gently roll the egg through the paint by tipping the pan.

Results:

1. A beautiful, colored edible egg.

2. A painted paper art.

Spot Design Painting

3 + years

Materials Needed:

White construction paper
Water colors
Cans of water
Sponges
Paint brushes

Procedure:

1. Sponge paper on both sides with water.

2. Load paint brush with paint and drip or "flick" color onto the paper.

3. Repeat using various colors.

4. Watch the colors blend.

Spray Bottle Painting

Materials Needed:

White construction paper
2-3 different colors of tempera paint
Paint brushes
Spray bottle filled with water
Optional:
Glue (thinned with water)
Glitter

Procedure:

1. Put paper on a flat surface.

2. Child will dip paint brush into desired color, then hold paint brush over paper and let the paint drip onto the paper.

3. The child can then spray the paint drops with water and watch the "paint streams" form on the paper.

Optional:

After the paint dries, child may want to drip glue onto the paper and sprinkle glitter.

Dangle and Swing Painting

Materials Needed:

Tape
Butcher paper
Paint brushes--various sizes
String
Paint

Procedure:

1. Tape a large piece of butcher paper onto the floor.

2. Tie strings around the handles of various-sized paint brushes.

3. Let child dip the brush into paint and then stand up, holding the string to let brush dangle and swing onto the paper.

Tissue Paper Paint

Materials Needed:

Tissue paper in a variety of colors
Paint brushes
Several clear containers of water
Paper

Procedure:

1. Let child tear the tissue paper into small pieces.

2. Put the torn tissue paper into containers of water to see what happens.

3. Stir with the paint brush.

4. After the water is colored, remove and discard the tissue paper and use colored water for paint.

5. Paint freely onto paper.

Mud Painting

3 1/2 + years

Materials Needed:

Sand sifter
Dirt
Large bowl for dirt
Containers for dirt
Water
Powdered tempera paint
Jumbo craft sticks
Paint brushes--sponge brushes
Base: matte board, cardboard, or something sturdy

Procedure:

1. Have child sift the dirt into a large bowl and separate dirt into several containers.

2. Add water and a small amount of powdered tempera to each and mix well.

3. Let child experiment freely with this medium. On a base, use paint brushes, sponge brushes, sticks, etc. Some may want to use the mud as finger paint.

4. If piled up, the mud may lend itself to a sculpture rather than a painting.

Note: Some may choose to keep the mud color rather than adding tempera.

Water Colors--a Different Approach

Materials Needed:

White paper
Sponge
Water colors
Paint brushes
Containers of water

Procedure:

1. Use sponge to wet the entire paper.

2. Let child paint freely with the water colors onto the wet paper.

3. Help child learn how to clean the brushes each time and use lots of water and paint.

Fun with Water Colors

Materials Needed:

Thick paper
Various brushes
Water
Watercolor paint
Masking tape
Rubbing alcohol
Eye droppers
Rock salt

Procedure:

1. Tape all edges of the paper to the table.

2. Brush water on the paper and make sure it's all wet.

3. Let child paint with water colors--any design--onto the paper.

4. Let child immediately drip on the rubbing alcohol with the eye droppers and sprinkle with the salt.

5. Watch what happens.

6. When paint is completely dry, wipe off the salt.

Egg Yolk Painting

Materials Needed:

Eggs
Bowls
Food coloring
Paper
Paint brush

Procedure:

1. Let child crack the egg and help him or her to separate the whites from the yolks.

2. Put the yolks into a bowl.

3. Add a few drops of food coloring to each egg yolk and mix.

4. The colors are bright, glossy and gorgeous.

5. Paint freely onto paper.

Variation: If you want to add glitter, buttons, etc., the yolk is sticky and no glue is necessary.

Homemade Paint

Materials Needed:

Small container with a lid
Teaspoons
Vinegar
Cornstarch
Food coloring

Mixture:

1/2 teaspoons vinegar
1/2 teaspoons cornstarch
10 drops food coloring

1. Put vinegar, corn starch and food coloring in the container.

2. Shake. If too thick, add vinegar. If too thin, add cornstarch.

Procedure:

1. Use as you would tempera paint.

Spinning Pictures

Materials Needed:

Salad spinner
Tempera
Spoons
Paper
Glitter (optional)

Procedure:

1. Cut paper to fit into the bottom of the salad spinner. Put the paper in the spinner.

2. Child drips paint onto the paper with a spoon.

3. Child puts lid on the salad spinner and spins. (This requires some degree of coordination and some children may need help.)

4. Sprinkle glitter on picture if desired.

Pendulum Painting

Materials Needed:

Small, soft plastic funnel
Large sheet of paper
Liquid starch
Powdered tempera
Strong string
Scissors
Small pitcher

Preparation Procedure:

1. Tie a string around the lip of the funnel (large end). Tie three pieces of string of equal lengths equally spaced to the string that is around the lip. Tie the three ends of the string together, approximately 12 inches from the top of the funnel.

2. Mix liquid starch and powdered tempera in pitcher. The paint should flow smoothly but not too fast.

3. Place a large sheet of paper on the floor or the ground.

Procedure:

1. Have child hold the pendulum over the paper. Place the tip of your finger over the hole in the funnel while the child pours the paint in.

2. Remove your finger and give the funnel a push.

3. Tell child to keep the pendulum movement going until all paint has run out of the funnel.

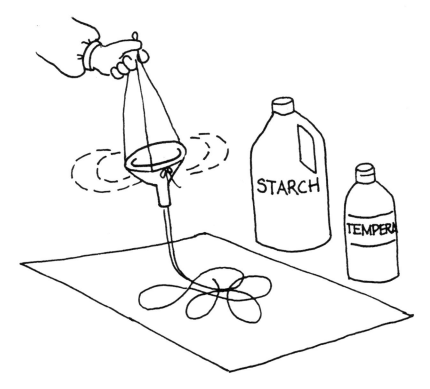

Shaker Painting

Materials Needed:

Thick paper or tagboard--cut in shapes or patterns (hearts, trees,
stars, triangles, circles, etc.)
Scissors
Glue (thinned with water)
Bowls for glue
Water
Brushes
Salt shakers with large holes
Powdered tempera*
Glitter

Procedure:

1. Let child paint the entire pattern with watered down glue.

2. Put powdered tempera and glitter into salt shakers.

3. Let child shake the mixture onto the glue.

Note: This takes a long time to dry.

* Powdered tempera is not recommended for use by children because of the
possibility of inhalation, however, we let our kids use scarfs or doctors's masks
tied around their noses. They love this part.

Black Line Design

Materials Needed:

White construction paper
Black liquid tempera
Bright-colored liquid tempera
Paint brushes
Containers

Procedure:

1. Ask child to paint lines in black on the white paper. Start from the middle of
the paper and make the lines go off the edge of the paper.

2. Let this dry.

3. Now paint inside the black lines with bright, shiny colors.

Note: It's fun to use the shiny paints mentioned in this book (page 17 or page 98.)

Tissue Paper Stain

Materials Needed:

Tissue paper (3-4 different colors torn into small pieces)
Base: matte board, cardboard, or other sturdy material
Paint brushes
Spray bottles
Water containers
Water

Procedure:

1. Give child a piece of base material.

2. Put a pile of torn tissue paper on the table in front of child. Let child choose pieces--as many or as few as desired--and place them on the base material.

3. Let child paint water all over the tissue pieces (the spray bottle or the paint brush can be used.)

4. Let child peel off the tissue paper and see the paint stain design.

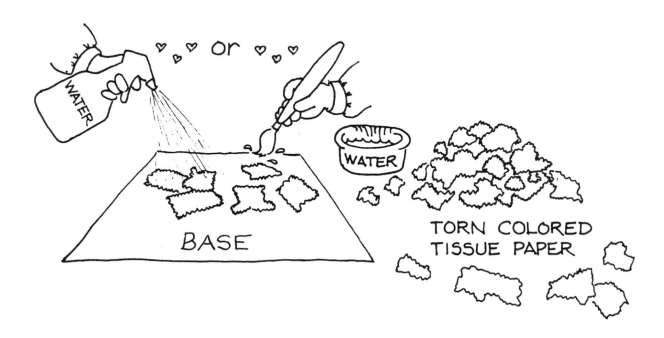

Homemade Bubbles

Materials Needed:

Powdered tempera
Water
Liquid starch
Detergent
Container for bubble mixture
Measuring cup

Mixture:

2 cups powdered tempera
1 cup water
1/2 cup liquid starch
1 cup liquid detergent

1. Stir powdered tempera with water until smooth. (Liquid tempera can be used.)

2. Add liquid starch and detergent. Mix.

3. Add additional water if needed to make the consistency of thin liquid soap.

Procedure:

1. Use as you would for store bought bubble mixture (Bubble Blowing Painting, page 25.)

Cellophane See-through Murals

Materials Needed:

Large sheets of colored cellophane (available on rolls)
Masking tape
Tempera paint
Bowls for paint
Paint brushes

Procedure:

1. Tape large sheets of cellophane to the window or sliding glass door.

2. The child can now paint with tempera onto the cellophane.

3. See the translucent design.

Nuts and Bolts Painting

Materials Needed:

Shallow box (large enough for paper to fit into)
Paper (cut to size of bottom of box)
2-3 colors of paint
Various sizes of nuts and bolts
Tape
Plastic spoons

Procedure:

1. Tape the paper to the bottom of the box.

2. Let child select some nuts and bolts. He or she may want to screw some of them (or all) together to create an interesting effect.

3. Let child spoon his or her choice of paint onto the paper.

4. The child can now drop the nuts and bolts into the box and roll them around in the paint (see Egg Roll Painting, page 12.)

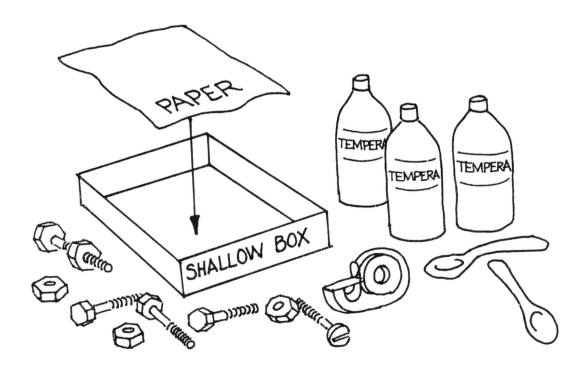

Raindrop Painting

Materials Needed:

Salt shakers
Powdered tempera (2 - 3 colors)
White construction paper or light-colored base material
Rain, or spray bottles filled with water

Procedure:

1. Put powdered tempera into salt shakers. (See * note on page 20.)

2. Let child shake dry tempera onto white paper or base. Use several colors.

3. Be careful not to spill the powdered paint. Put paper or base outside in the rain. See the dry paint turn into a painting.

Variations: 1) If it does not rain, use spray bottles filled with water. 2) Run an ice cube over the dry paint and see the colors appear. 3) Leave the dry painting outside overnight and let the dew create a new picture for the child to see the next day (must be done with a heavier weight base.)

Painting with Paste

Materials Needed:

Paste
Liquid tempera (several colors)
Craft sticks
Base: matte board, cardboard, or other sturdy material
Measuring spoons
Containers for paint mixture
Mixing spoons

Mixture:

2 tablespoons paste
2 tablespoons liquid tempera

1. Mix.

Procedure:

1. Mix several colors of this mixture.

2. Use craft sticks to "paint" with this mixture. It will create a textured effect.

Variation: Beads, bangles, sticks, rocks, shells, etc. can be added for a different effect.

Bubble Blowing Painting

Materials Needed:

Containers of bubble mixture
(see Homemade Bubbles, page 22)
Bubble wands or gadgets to use as wands--strawberry basket, potato masher,
whisk, plastic 6-pack rings, toilet paper tubes, funnels, spools, etc.
White paper
Food coloring

Procedure:

1. Squeeze a lot of food coloring into bubble mixture.

2. Let child dip the wand into the colored bubble mixture and then blow the
bubbles onto the paper.

Variation: It's fun to blow, chase, and pop the bubbles with the paper.

Homemade Water Colors

Materials Needed:

Liquid or powdered tempera
Water
Small containers--such as ones used for sauces in fast food restaurants
Mixing spoons

Procedure:

1. Mix the powdered tempera with water or use the liquid tempera and pour into a small container.

2. Let this dry for several days until it is hard, or put it in the microwave for one minute and then let completely dry.

3. Use as watercolors.

Tile Painting

2 + years

Materials Needed:

White tiles
Permanent felt markers
Aprons

Procedure:

1. Let child draw freely onto plain white tiles with permanent felt markers.

Note: These markers will stain clothes, so an apron is advised.

Homemade Fabric Paint

3 + years

If you do not have commercial fabric paints, you can simply use food coloring diluted with water.

Paint the Snow

Materials Needed:

Food coloring or liquid tempera paint
Paint brushes of various sizes
Snow
Containers

Procedure:

1. Mix food coloring and water and put into containers or use liquid tempera paint.

2. Take outside and let child paint the snow.

Variation: Powdered tempera can be used with snow and it will mix to create paint.

27

Felt Pen Spray Painting

Materials Needed:

Felt pens--all colors
Absorbent paper--paper towels, coffee filters, etc.
Spray bottles filled with water

Procedure:

1. Let child draw freely with felt pens onto absorbent paper.

2. Spray the felt pen drawing with water and see the colors blend.

Crayons

Note: Some crayons are supplemented with chalk. These are identified by their lack of liquidity when attempting to melt them.

Melted Crayon Pictures

Materials Needed:

Crayons--all different sizes and kinds
Base: matte board, cardboard, felt, paper, balsa wood, or other sturdy material
Metal tray or baking sheet
Aluminum foil, or small foil dish
Rocks, shells, sticks, etc. (Optional)
Hot sunny day
Oven

Procedure:

1. Ask child to peel the paper from the crayons.

2. Cover the baking sheet with aluminum foil.

3. Have child place the base material on the tray.

4. Let child place his or her peeled crayons anywhere on the base material. In a pile, stacked or randomly is fine.

5. **Optional:** Offer rocks, shells, etc. to place in, around and under the pile of crayons.

6. Just leave to melt in the hot sun or place tray in a 250° oven for about 10 minutes and supervise.

7. Child may want to push and pull melted crayons before they cool.

Note: Children enjoy watching this transformation.

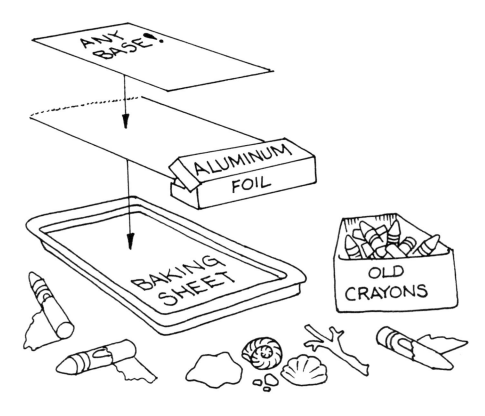

Multi-colored Crayon Making

Materials Needed:

Colored crayons
Double boiler, or griddle lined with aluminum foil
Metal cup
Candy mold, muffin tin, ice cube trays, or other molds
Pot holder

Procedure:

1. Place one color of crayon into a metal cup in the double boiler or griddle and melt the crayon(s) until it is liquid crayon.

2. Take this liquid and pour a thin layer into a mold. Let it cool.

3. Melt another color of crayon and pour this on top of the first color. Let this cool.

4. Continue until you have as many colors as you want. This will create a layered crayon.

5. Pop out of mold when completely cool.

Variation: For a swirled effect, melt two crayon colors at a time, but do not mix together.

See-through Drawings

3 + years

Materials Needed:

White paper
Crayons
Baby oil or cooking oil
Cotton balls
Newspaper

Procedure:

1. Place white paper onto newspaper.

2. Let child draw freely with crayon onto the white paper. Ask him or her to press hard.

3. When the drawing is completed, use a cotton ball and rub a small amount of oil over the back of the paper.

4. Let this oil design dry on newspaper.

Note: The oil makes the drawing transparent.

Melted Crayon Shavings

Materials Needed:

Peeled crayons
Assorted colored paper, foil, sandpaper, or waxed paper
Potato peelers, cheese grater, or pencil sharpener
Warming tray or griddle

Procedure:

1. On colored paper, foil, sandpaper, or waxed paper, let child shave, peel, cut, sharpen or crush crayons.

2. Place paper and shavings on the warming tray or griddle and watch the colors melt.

3. Take paper off the tray or griddle and watch the colors cool.

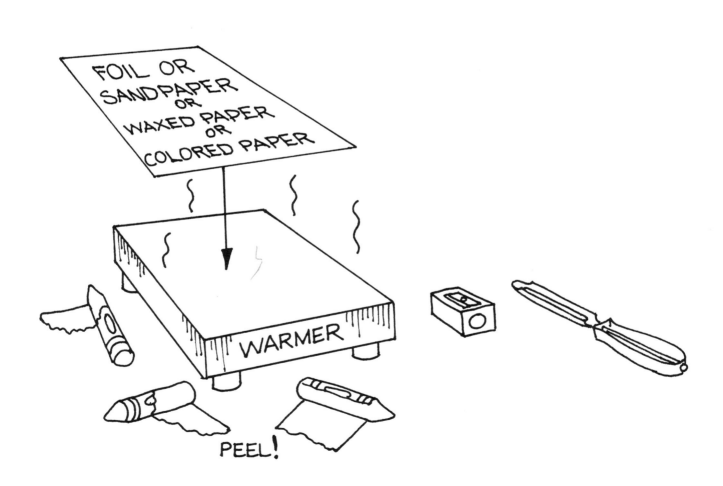

Snow Painting

Materials Needed:

Dark construction paper (red, blue, purple)
Crayons
Paint brushes
Epsom salt
Hot water
Containers
Measuring cups and spoons

Mixture:

1/4 cup hot water
4 tablespoons Epsom salt

1. Stir to dissolve.

Procedure:

1. Let child draw freely with crayons onto the paper.

2. When completed, brush the drawing with salt mixture.

3. Let dry. Snowy effect!!

Melted Crayon Printing

Materials Needed:

Gadgets to use for printing--unifix cubes, cookie cutters, stamps, potato
    masher, etc.
Peeled crayons
Muffin tin, aluminum pans, or metal cup
Assorted colored paper
Warming tray or griddle

Procedure:

1. Put one color of crayon into the muffin tins, aluminum pans, or metal cup and
   place on the warming tray or griddle.

2. Let the crayons melt completely until you have liquefied crayons.

3. Place gadgets into the liquid crayons and quickly stamp onto the paper. Child
   will need to stamp quickly or the crayon will harden.

Note: CAUTION! This requires a 1 to 1 adult to child ratio for supervision
because liquid crayons become very hot.

Melted Crayons onto Sandpaper

Materials Needed:

Electric griddle or warming tray
Crayons (peeled)
Sandpaper (medium grade)
Thick, dry sponges

Procedure:

1. Turn griddle to 380° and then turn down to 275° to keep warm.

2. Give child a piece of sandpaper.

3. Place sandpaper on the griddle or tray.

4. Let child place his or her non-drawing hand on a thick, dry sponge to protect against burns while holding the sandpaper down.

5. Rub the peeled crayon over the sandpaper and slowly see and feel it melt. If it does not melt easily, raise the heat a bit.

Melted Crayon and Sandpaper Print

Materials Needed:

Sandpaper (medium grade)
Crayons
Iron
White paper

Procedure:

1. Let child draw freely with crayon onto the sandpaper. Press hard.

2. When finished, take a sheet of white paper and place over the sandpaper.

3. With a fairly hot iron, let the child iron the white paper onto the sandpaper.

4. Presto--you now have a sandpaper print **and** the original sandpaper drawing.

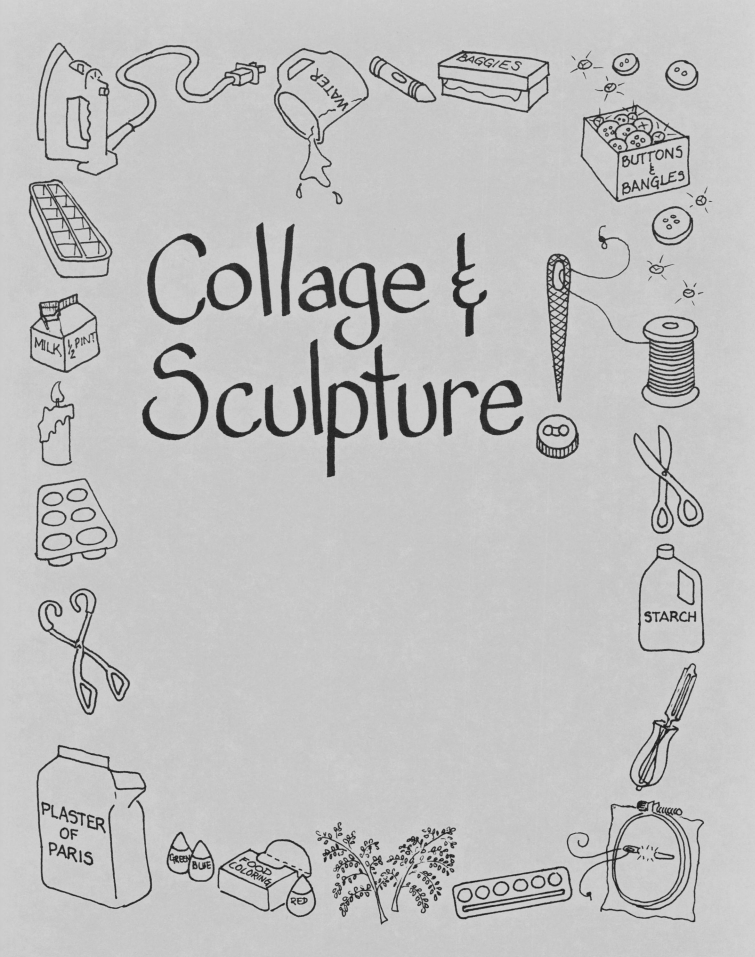

Collage & Sculpture!

Sandwiched Collage

Materials Needed:

Newspaper or cardboard
Iron
Waxed paper
Construction paper
Cellophane
Photograph mounting paper (available at camera stores) cut to size of construction paper
Ferns (dry and flat)
Tissue paper, wrapping paper

Procedure:

1. Place cardboard or newspaper on hard surface.

2. Place a piece of construction paper onto the cardboard or newspaper.

3. Then place colored cellophane onto the construction paper.

4. Let child lay out the dried ferns, and perhaps some tissue or wrapping paper (face down).

5. Place a piece of photograph mounting paper over the cellophane and dried fern design.

6. Cover the whole thing with a piece of waxed paper.

7. Run an iron, which is set on low heat--no steam--over the waxed paper. Press down and heat as long as it takes to adhere, mounting the paper--about 30 seconds to a minute.

8. Let cool, and remove the construction paper. Turn over and trim excess waxed paper. BEAUTIFUL!

   Note: If you have the paper cut ahead of time, the child can do most of this him or herself with your help.

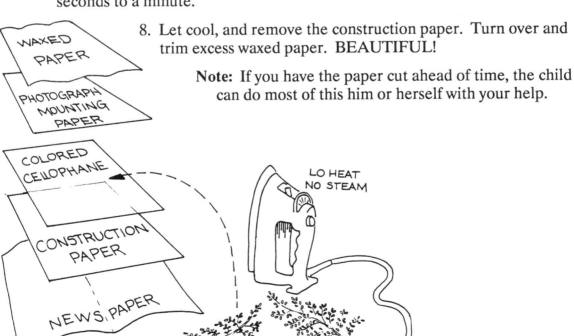

Smelly Collage

Materials Needed:

Collect items that have a scent:
  Lipstick and make-up
  Perfume
  Spices
  Potpourri
  Food extracts
  Coffee grinds
  Gum
  Toothpaste
  Soap
Tissues or paper towels
Glue
Base: matte board, cardboard, or other sturdy material

Procedure:

1. Assemble materials in any order on the table.

2. Let child glue onto the base any materials that can be glued, in any arrangement desired.

3. Draw with the lipstick. Tissues can be used for the liquid items like perfume or make-up and then glued down.

4. Let dry and SMELL!!

Egg Carton Sculpture

3 1/2 + years

Materials Needed:

Egg cartons cut up
Base: Matte board, cardboard, or other sturdy material
Glue
Paint
Paint brushes

Procedure:

1. Cut the cup portion of the egg carton into individual cups.

2. Let child freely glue these cups onto a base.

3. This can be painted when the glue is dry.

Sewing on Burlap

Materials Needed:

Burlap
Big sewing needles (threaded)
Bangles
Buttons
Fabric scraps
Thread
Embroidery hoops

Procedures:

1. Let child freely sew on the burlap.

2. Bangles, fabric, buttons, etc. can be added to the creation.

3. Tie off thread for the child.

Note: An embroidery hoop helps to hold the burlap tight and steady.

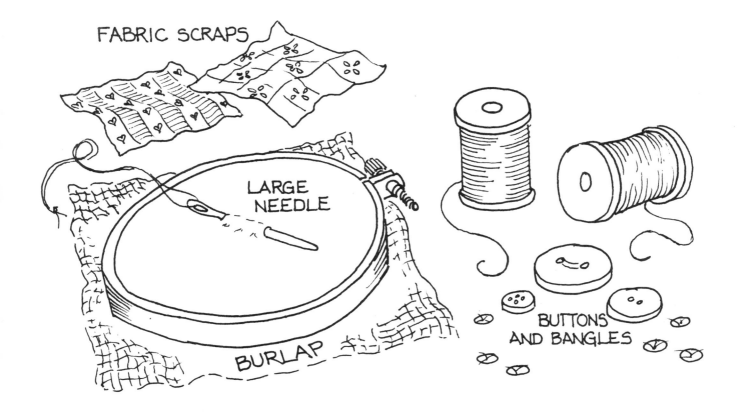

FABRIC SCRAPS

LARGE NEEDLE

BURLAP

BUTTONS AND BANGLES

Collage Fruit Seeds

2 1/2 + years

Materials Needed:

All types of fruit seeds--melons, pumpkins, apples, oranges, papaya, peaches, plums, etc.
Glue
Glue brushes
Base: matt board, cardboard, paper plates, or other sturdy material

Procedure:

1. Child can freely glue the various fruit seeds onto the base.

Note: This is great for language development. Discuss the various kinds of fruits from which the seeds come. Real fruit or pictures would enhance this experience.

Ice Sculpture

2 + years

Materials Needed:

Water table or deep basin
30 - 50 lbs. of ice cubes (approximately 5 bags of store-bought cubed ice)
Food coloring
Rock salt
Eye droppers
Containers of water

Procedure:

1. Dump ice cubes into the water table.

2. Pour some rock salt over the ice.

3. Place containers of water mixed with food coloring and eye droppers around the table.

4. Let child drop and drip color onto the ice to create beautiful ice designs. Watch the new colors emerge.

Plaster Sculpture

Materials Needed:

Plaster of Paris or spackling powder
Water bowls
Styrofoam, shredded paper, sawdust, or other material that will give plaster bulk
Base: matte board, cardboard, or other sturdy material
Spoons
Measuring cup

Mixture:

1 cup dry plaster of Paris
1/2 cup water

1. Mix together.

Procedure:

1. Mix plaster and let child add styrofoam, shredded paper, sawdust or anything that will give the plaster bulk.

2. Give each child a base to work on. With spoon, let him or her scoop the plaster onto the base and arrange it any manner.

3. This sets quickly.

Note: These can be painted with liquid tempera when dry.

Confetti Collage

Materials Needed:

Confetti--different colors
Bowls for each color
Colored construction paper
Glitter
Cotton swab and tooth picks
Scissors
Glue
Hole punch
White paper or base material: matte board, cardboard, or other sturdy material

Procedure:

1. While the teacher may want to have some confetti already on hand, it's fun for the children to help make more. There are two ways to do this.

   a. Let child use a hole punch and punch holes into construction paper. The holes become the confetti.

   b. Cut construction paper into thin strips, and then let child cut or tear the strips to make confetti.

2. Let child choose colors of confetti and put them into a bowl. Mix with the toothpick.

3. Use the cotton swab to make a design on the paper with the glue.

4. Sprinkle with confetti and glitter.

5. Shake off the excess and let dry.

Sea Life Collage

Materials Needed:

Blue base material (to symbolize the ocean): matte board,
   paper or plastic plates, plastic, styrofoam meat trays, etc.
Glue
Glue brushes
Beach items--sea weed, feathers, shells, sand, driftwood, starfish, sand dollars,
   corks, etc.

Procedure:

1. Let the child glue the sea items in any design desired onto the base.

Free Form Plastic Bag Sculpture

Materials Needed:

Plaster of Paris
Water
Spoons to scoop plaster of Paris into measuring cup
Measuring cup
Thick, sturdy, plastic sandwich-sized bags
Twist ties

Procedure:

1. Give each child a plastic bag, some dry plaster of Paris and water.

2. Each child will measure 1 cup of plaster of Paris and 1/2 cup of water into the bag.

3. Be sure to put the twist tie onto the bag.

4. Let child knead, roll, punch, poke, etc. the bag with the mixture in it. As he or she works with it, it will start to set.

5. When it is hard, remove the bag to reveal a unique free form sculpture.

Note: These can be painted with liquid tempera.

Paper Tube Sculpture

Materials Needed:

Paper tubes from paper towels, toilet paper, wrapping paper
Glue
Scissors
Hole punches
Base: matte board, cardboard, or other sturdy material
Straws

Preparation Procedure:

1. Cut the tubes into various lengths and cut designs into them. Use hole punches. Cut spirals, cut negative space, etc.

Procedure:

1. Let child arrange and connect these tubes as desired using lots of glue.

2. The tubes can be stacked, fit inside of each other, used as bridges, etc.

Variation: Straws can be added to create a different look.

Bone Sculpture

Materials Needed:

Bones (chicken, steak and turkey bones)
Base: matte board, cardboard, heavy paper, or other sturdy material
Glue
Glue brushes

Preparation Procedure:

1. Boil chicken, turkey or beef bones.

2. Drain and place in an oven or microwave for a few minutes until dry and clean.

Procedure:

1. Let child freely create any collage or sculpture with the bones.

Mud Brick Sculpture

Materials Needed for Bricks:

Dirt
Water
Mixing bowl
Ice cube trays and or muffin tins

Procedure for Making Bricks:

1. Put dirt into the bowl.

2. Add some water.

3. Mix the mud until you can make it into a ball.

4. Press the mud into an ice cube tray or muffin tin.

5. Put the trays in a warm place.

6. Let the bricks dry for about 10 days or bake in 250° oven for 15 minutes.

7. Then, do the drop test. Slip a brick out of the tray. Drop it onto the floor. If it doesn't break, the bricks are dry enough.

Materials Needed for Sculpture:

Mud bricks
Rocks, pebbles
Wood
Sticks
Leaves
Nature treasures
Mud, plaster of Paris (runny), or spackling powder

Procedure:

1. Allow the child to freely explore and build using the various materials.

2. The mud or plaster of Paris can be used to stick the materials together.

3. Let dry.

Computer Paper Side Strip Sculpture

Materials Needed:

Perforated side strips off of computer paper--various lengths
Food coloring
Water
Liquid starch
Glue
Bowls
Glue brushes
Base: matte board, cardboard, or other sturdy material

Procedure:

1. Let child dye strips of paper with food coloring. Use a small amount of water and a lot of food coloring. Mix around in a bowl until the color dyes the paper. If you want the paper to be a little stiff, put some liquid starch into the water and food coloring mixture.

2. Let the strips dry completely.

3. Have child glue strips to base. These can be built up, piled, and connected.

4. Let dry.

Wax Sculpture

Materials Needed:

Crayons
Old candles
Aluminum pie or muffin tins
Hot plate or griddle
Flat pan and water
Pail of ice water
Gloves (rubber)
Tongs
Potato peeler, cheese grater, or pencil sharpener

Procedure:

1. Have child shave some crayons and place the shavings in either the muffin tin or the aluminum pie tin with chunks of candles. **Do not fill to full.**

2. These tins should go inside a flat pan of water to avoid overheating.

3. Place flat pan on the hot plate or griddle until the wax has melted.

4. Put on the gloves. Grasping the muffin or pie tin containing melted wax mixture with tongs, plunge the tin straight down into the pail of ice water.

5. The wax shoots up and hardens immediately.

6. Gently turn the wax upside down to let any water out.

Note: Be sure to stand back when you plunge the wax into the water. Pie tin will result in a large, broad sculpture, and muffin tins will result in several small, taller sculptures.

Colored Styrofoam and Toothpick Sculpture

Materials Needed:

Styrofoam--small bits
Colored toothpicks
Liquid tempera
Bowls
Spoons
Glue

Procedure:

1. Place styrofoam into various bowls and add liquid tempera. Let child stir this around until the styrofoam is colored. Let the styrofoam dry.

2. When these are dry, let child dip the ends of the toothpicks into glue and then into the styrofoam.

3. This will create a "Tinkertoy" kind of sculpture.

Note: When the glue dries, the sculpture will not fall apart and it can be picked up and taken home.

Tissue Collage

3 + years

Materials Needed:

Tissue paper scraps
Clear-drying white glue (thinned with water)
Base: matte board, cardboard, or other sturdy material
Markers (thick black water-based marker is best)
Paint brushes
Child-safe spray varnish or glue (thinned with water)

Procedure:

1. Let child apply the glue to the base using fingers or brushes.

2. Arrange the tissue in any design desired (overlapping may occur naturally; this is fine).

3. Allow the glue to dry for a few minutes.

4. Once dry, let child draw on the tissue paper with a marker.

5. Let dry and cover with a thin layer of glue or child-safe spray varnish to set it.

Wire Sculpture

Materials Needed:

Half pint empty milk cartons (one per child)
Plaster of Paris
Water
Coated electrical wire
Water colors and brushes
Bowl
Spoons
Measuring cups

Mixture:

2 cups of plaster of Paris
1 cup of water

1. Mix together. Makes enough for six milk cartons.

Procedure:

1. Pour plaster into the milk cartons.

2. As plaster begins to set, have child place wires into the plaster in any arrangement.

3. When the plaster is set, remove the milk carton by tearing it away from the plaster.

4. Child may then move the wires into any shape or sculpture.

Note: The plaster base may then be painted.

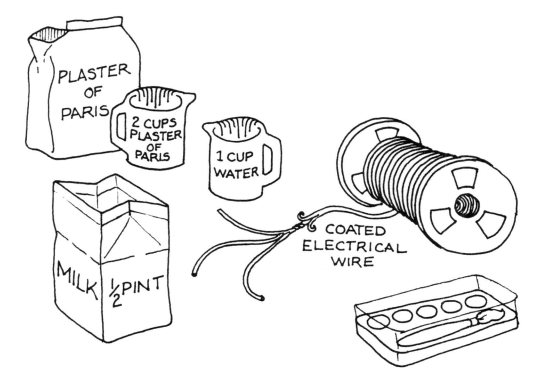

Frozen Balloon Sculpture

Materials Needed:

Balloons--various shapes and sizes
Water
Freezer
Water table or large bin
Eye droppers
Food coloring or water color

Procedure:

1. Day One

   a. Fill each balloon with water and place in the freezer for at least 24 hours.

2. Day Two

   a. When the water in the balloon is completely frozen, tear away the balloon. You will see balloon shapes of ice.

   b. Place ice balloons into a water table or large bin.

   c. Let the children surround the bin and drop food coloring or water color onto the ice balloons.

   d. This is a group project and will create a beautiful ice sculpture. As the balloons melt, the colors run and drip, creating a new and unusual effect.

Variation: This can also be done as an individual project where each child gets one balloon to work with. This will require lots of freezer space.

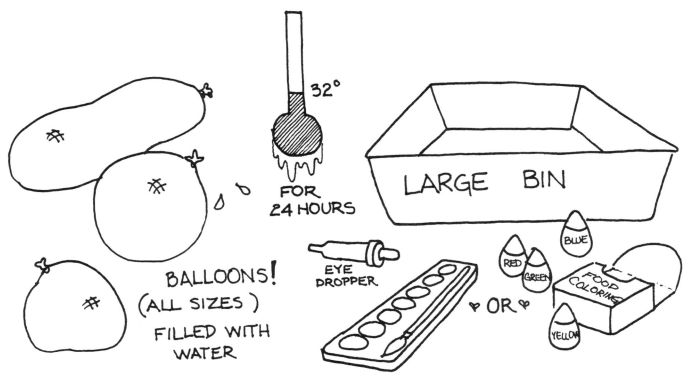

54

Modeling Mixtures

Toothpaste Putty

Materials Needed:

Toothpaste (creamy, not gel)
White glue
Measuring spoons
Cornstarch
Water
Small dish

Mixture:

1/2 teaspoon toothpaste
1 tablespoon white glue
2 tablespoons cornstarch
1/2 teaspoon water

1. Mix toothpaste, glue and cornstarch in a dish.

2. Add water.

3. Mix until it's putty-like.

Procedure:

1. Let child push, pull, roll and play freely.

Note: Putty begins to dry in 20 minutes, so to soften it, use a drop of water. This will dry hard in 24 hours.

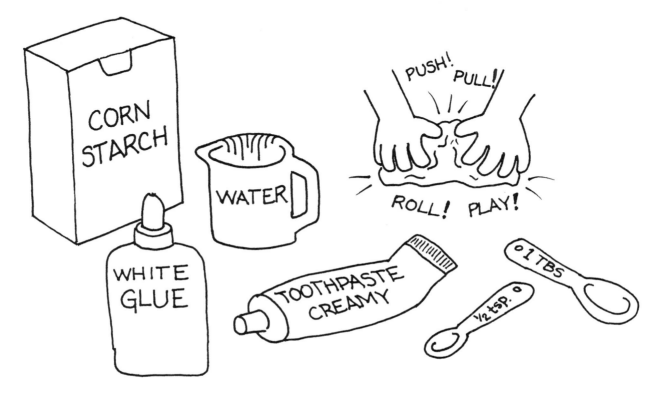

Fundough

Materials Needed:

Flour
Salt
Water
Food coloring
Oil
Vinegar
Bowls
Measuring cups and spoons
Mixing spoons

Mixture:

3 cups flour
1 cup salt
1 cup water plus food coloring
1/4 cup oil
2 tablespoons vinegar

1. Mix all ingredients well. Add more water if necessary. Knead.

Procedure:

1. Let child play freely with the dough.

Note: This dough keeps indefinitely in a plastic bag. Dampen occasionally, working water into the dough as it dries out.

Kool Aid Play Dough

Materials Needed:

Flour
Boiling water
Salt
Unsweetened Kool Aid Drink Mix
Oil
Bowl
Measuring cups and spoons
Mixing spoons

Mixture:

2 1/2 cups flour
1 cup salt
3 teaspoons oil
2 cups boiling water
2 packages Kool Aid

1. Mix the dry ingredients.

2. Add water and oil. Knead.

Procedure:

1. Play freely

Note: The color and smell of this dough are delightful!

raffin Modeling Mixture

Materials Needed:

Paraffin
Hot plate
Metal container
Crayon or chalk shavings
Potato peeler, cheese grater, or pencil sharpener to make shavings
Water--warm and cold
Pot holder

Procedure:

1. Melt paraffin in metal container on hot plate on low heat.

2. Add crayon or chalk shavings to the liquid paraffin.

3. Melt down and let cool.

4. When mixture is cool but still soft, let child model with it.

Note: Dipping hands in warm water from time to time will keep mixture soft. Use cold water to harden and polish the paraffin sculpture.

Salt and Starch Modeling Mixture

Materials Needed:

Salt
Cornstarch
Water
Paint
Double boiler
Waxed paper or cookie sheet
Measuring cups
Spoons

Mixture:

1 cup salt
1/2 cup cornstarch
3/4 cup cold water

1. Mix salt and cornstarch in the top of the double boiler

2. Add cold water slowly.

3. Stir mixture.

4. Place over boiling water stirring constantly until the mixture has thickened and is difficult to stir.

5. Spoon onto waxed paper or cookie sheet to cool.

6. Knead it a bit to take out the air bubbles and lumps.

Procedure:

1. Let child freely model with it.

Note: These will dry and child can paint it when dry. When not using, roll into ball and wrap well in waxed paper. It will remain soft for several days.

Javadoh

Materials Needed:

Dried, used coffee grounds
Flour
Water
Bowl
Food coloring or tempera
Mixing spoons

Mixture:

1. Mix 1 part used coffee grounds (dried) to 2 parts flour in a bowl. Add water and extra flour to desired consistency.

2. If color is desired, add a few drops of food coloring or tempera.

Procedure:

1. Let child manipulate as desired. Notice the texture.

Modeling Dough

Materials Needed:

Flour
Salt
Powdered alum or oil of cloves (both items available at a pharmacy)
Vegetable oil
Boiling water
Food coloring or tempera paint
Measuring cups and spoons
Mixing spoons
Paint
Paint brushes

Mixture:

3/4 cup flour
1/2 cup salt
1 1/2 teaspoons powdered alum or oil of cloves
1 1/2 teaspoons vegetable oil
1/2 cup boiling water

1. Mix flour, salt and alum or oil of cloves in mixing bowl.

2. Add vegetable oil and boiling water.

3. Stir vigorously with a spoon until well-blended.

4. Dough should not stick to the sides of the bowl and should be cool enough to handle.

5. Add food coloring or tempera paint and knead into the dough.

Procedure:

1. Let child make a creation.

2. Let dry over night.

3. Paint when dry.

Sand Dough

Materials Needed:

Sand
Hot water
Cornstarch
Alum (available at a pharmacy)
Bowl
Saucepan
Hot plate or stove
Measuring cups and spoons
Mixing spoons
Food coloring (optional)

Mixture:

3 cups sand
2 1/4 cups hot water
1 1/2 cups cornstarch
3 teaspoons alum
Food coloring (optional)

1. Mix sand, cornstarch, and alum in a saucepan.

2. Add hot water, and food coloring if desired.

3. Cook over medium heat until thickened.

4. Remove from heat and knead until smooth.

Procedure:

1. Play freely.

Note: Store in an airtight container. This will dry.

Grated Cheese Modeling Dough

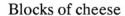

Materials Needed:

Blocks of cheese
Cheese grater
Bowl
Mayonnaise
Flour
Waxed paper
Bowls of breadcrumbs, granola, nuts, or other edible items for texture

Procedure:

1. Child may grate the cheese.

2. Mix 1/4 to 1/2 cup grated cheese in a bowl with 1/2 teaspoon mayonnaise.

3. Add a pinch of flour and mix to desired consistency.

4. Give each child a piece of waxed paper and his or her lump of cheese dough. Model freely.

5. Cheese mixture can be rolled in bread crumbs, granola, paprika, nuts or whatever for variation and texture. (If this is to be eaten, eat immediately or refrigerate.)

Note: Mayonnaise should not be unrefrigerated for any longer than 2 hours.

Craft Clay

Materials Needed:

Cornstarch
Baking soda
Water
Food coloring
Measuring cups
Mixing spoons
Hot plate or stove
Saucepan
Cookie sheet
Glue (thinned with water)
Paint brushes
Liquid tempera

Mixture:

1 cup cornstarch
2 cups baking soda
1 1/4 cup water
Food coloring

1. Combine ingredients in a saucepan.

2. Cook over medium heat, stirring continuously.

3. Dump onto cookie sheet to cool.

4. Knead while cooling.

Procedure:

1. When cool, let child model with it freely.

2. This will harden and can be painted. A final coat of watered-down glue will give it a shine.

Note: Store in foil or in an airtight container.

Modeling Rice

Materials Needed:

Long grain rice
Water
Measuring cups and spoons
Food coloring
Mixing spoons
Hot plate or stove
Saucepan

Mixture:

1 cup long grain rice
3 cups water
1 teaspoon food coloring

1. Bring water to boil in saucepan.

2. Add rice and food coloring.

3. Cover and simmer on low heat for 15 minutes.

4. Uncover and continue cooking for 10 minutes, stirring occasionally.

5. Cool and use.

Procedure:

1. Let child explore freely.

Note: Store covered in the refrigerator.

No Cook Mint Patties

Materials Needed:

Light corn syrup
Butter or margarine
Peppermint extract
Salt
Powdered sugar
Food coloring if desired
Measuring cups and spoons
Mixing bowl
Small bowls
Mixing spoons

Mixture:

1/3 cup light corn syrup
1/4 cup butter or margarine
1 teaspoon peppermint extract
1/2 teaspoon salt
1 lb. powdered sugar

1. Mix all ingredients except the food coloring in mixing bowl.

2. Divide the mixture into separate bowls.

3. Using food coloring, make each mixture a different color. Mix.

Procedure:

1. Create your own design with the various colors of dough.

Note: These can be eaten but they are VERY SWEET.

Sand Sculptures

Materials Needed:

Water
Plaster of Paris
Sand
Waxed paper
Mixing bowl
Mixing spoons
Liquid tempera
Paint brushes

Procedure:

1. Mix water and plaster of Paris together in mixing bowl until it looks like cream.

2. Quickly stir in the sand until it looks like thick whipped cream.

3. Pour some onto waxed paper, creating gullies, valleys and hills. Squeeze and push it to make designs.

4. This dries very quickly (about 5 minutes). Paint when dry.

Cloud Dough

Materials Needed:

Flour
Powdered tempera
Salad oil
Water
Measuring cups and spoons
Bowl

Mixture:

3 cups flour
2 tablespoons powdered tempera
1/2 cup salad oil
Water

1. Mix together the flour, tempera, and oil.

2. Add enough water to make a soft, pliable, elastic-like dough.

Procedure:

1. Play freely.

Chalk Screening

Materials Needed:

Large, colored construction paper
Cornstarch
Water
Paint brush
Wire screening--small mesh
Chalk
Stencils or patterns or leaves, etc.
Containers for paint

Procedure:

1. Fill paint container 1/3 full with cornstarch and water. Mix. **This should be very liquid.**

2. Paint cornstarch mixture onto construction paper.

3. Place wire mesh screen on top of construction paper.

4. Draw with chalk on top of the wire mesh.

Note: Cornstarch mixture will allow the chalk to adhere to the paper.

Variation: Stencils or patterns can be placed between the cornstarch mixture and mesh to create a negative print.

Chalk Painting

Materials Needed:

Colored chalk
Small sponges or paint brushes
Water
Paper
Potato peeler, cheese grater, or pencil sharpener
Containers for chalk
Small bowls of water

Procedure:

1. Finely grate colored chalk into separate containers (children love to do this.) Each container should hold one color.

2. Supply each child with a piece of paper, a bowl of water and a variety of small sponges.

3. Let child dip his or her sponge into the water, then into the desired color of grated chalk, and paint freely onto the paper.

Note: The colors will mix and change as child continues to paint.

Condensed Chalk Presentation

3 + years

Materials Needed:

Colored chalk
Sweetened condensed milk
White construction paper
Bowl for sweetened condensed milk
Paint brushes

Procedure:

1. Pour sweetened condensed milk into bowl.

2. Paint the entire paper with the sweetened condensed milk.

3. Draw on the wet paper with the colored chalk.

Note: See the shine.

Chalk and Tempera

Materials Needed:

Colored chalk
White tempera paint
Paper
Paint brushes

Procedure:

1. Let child make a colored chalk drawing on the piece of paper. Be sure child presses down hard with the chalk.

2. Take another piece of paper of the same size and brush white tempera over the entire surface.

3. While the paint is still wet, place the chalk drawing face down on the painted paper and press.

4. Lift off the top piece and see the results.

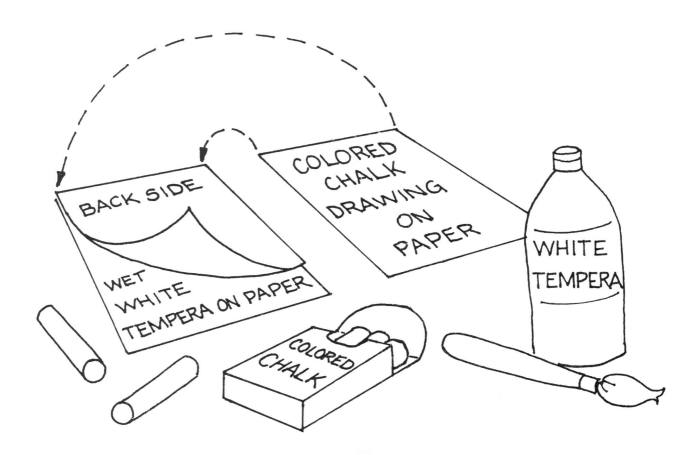

Chalk Presentation

Materials Needed:

Sandpaper--medium to fine grade
Colored chalk
Small bowls for glue
White glue (thinned with water)

Procedure:

1. Pour glue into bowls.

2. Dip chalk into the glue and draw freely onto the sandpaper.

Note: See the shine.

Variation: Construction paper can be used instead of sandpaper.

Chalk and Bleach

Materials Needed:

Bleach
Aprons
Black construction paper
Chalk
Bowl of soapy water and towels to wash hands afterwards
Small bowls for bleach

Procedure:

1. Be sure that child wears an apron and is in a well-ventilated room. DO NOT LEAVE THIS UNATTENDED.

2. Let child dip the chalk into the bleach and then draw freely onto the paper.

3. Have child wash hands when finished.

Note: The effect is luminescent.

Grated Chalk and Stencils

Materials Needed:

Potato peeler, cheese grater, or pencil sharpener
Paper
Colored chalk
Wet sponge
Shakers with large holes
Waxed paper
Hair spray

Procedure:

1. Let child grate various colored chalk onto a piece of waxed paper.

2. Transfer grated chalk into shakers.

3. With a wet sponge child can wet the paper completely.

4. Then SHAKE-SHAKE-SHAKE the chalk onto the wet paper.

Note: Let the creations dry and when the children have left the room hair spray can be used to set the chalk if desired.

Variation: On heavier paper, child can paint a thin layer of water color onto the paper and then shake the chalk on.

Sponge and Chalk Prints

Materials Needed:

Wet sponges
Chalk
Paper

Procedure:

1. Child can draw freely on a wet sponge with chalk.

2. DAB-DAB-DAB the sponge onto a piece of paper and see the nice chalk print.

Cotton Swab Chalk Design

3 + years

Materials Needed:

Potato peeler, cheese grater, or pencil sharpener
Colored chalk
Cups, muffin tins, egg cartons, or any container to separate colors
Cotton swabs
Water in small bowls
Paper

Procedure:

1. Let child grate chalk into cups, muffin tins, egg cartons, or any container to separate the colors.

2. Child can then dip the cotton swab into the water, then into the chalk and draw freely using the swab as a paint brush.

Printing

STAMP PAD

RUBBER CEMENT

ALUMINUM FOIL

SMALL TILE

TEMPERA

WOOD

PLASTER OF PARIS

PAINT

Rubber Band Printing

Materials Needed:

Blocks (For better handling, corks can be hot glued onto the blocks to act as a handle.)
Rubber bands
Base: matte board, cardboard, or other sturdy material
Tempera powder (2-3 colors)
Liquid starch
Shallow paint container (pie plate works well) lined with paper towel
Spoon for spreading paint

Preparation Procedure:

1. Mix tempera and starch into a fairly thick paint.

2. Pour very small amount of this paint onto paper towel in shallow container, and spread with a spoon.

Procedure:

1. Let child wrap rubber bands around the block in any arrangement.

2. Have child dip the block into the paint and then press onto the base. Presto!

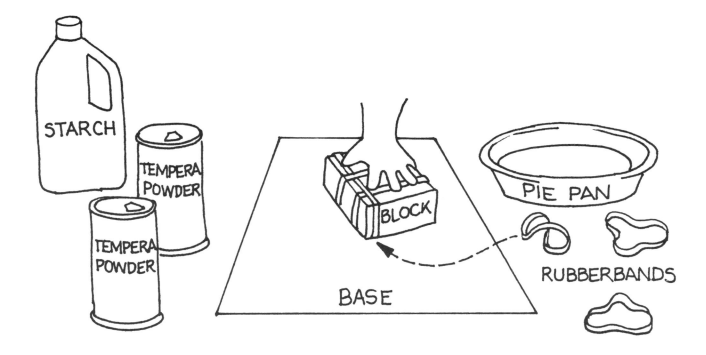

Can Roller

Materials Needed:

Tin cans
Heavy cotton string
Liquid tempera
Rubber cement
Paper
Masking tape
Shallow container for paint (pie plate works well) lined with paper towel
Spoon for spreading paint

Preparation Procedure:

1. Remove both ends of the tin can. Wash and dry the can and then place masking tape over the ends to prevent possible cuts.

2. Paint the can with rubber cement.

3. Wrap string around the can in various designs.

4. Let dry.

5. Pour a small amount of liquid tempera onto paper towel in shallow container, and spread with a spoon.

Procedure:

1. Let child roll the can into tempera paint and then roll it onto the paper.

Cellophane Tape Magic Print

Materials Needed:

Cellophane tape
Base: matte board, cardboard, or other sturdy material
Wet sponges
Chalk

Procedure:

1. The child can make a design onto the base by taping cellophane tape down in any pattern.

2. Let child draw onto the wet sponge with chalk in any design.

3. DAB, DAB, DAB the sponge onto the cellophane-taped paper. The chalk will adhere to the places where there is no tape.

4. Carefully remove the tape and you will see a negative space print.

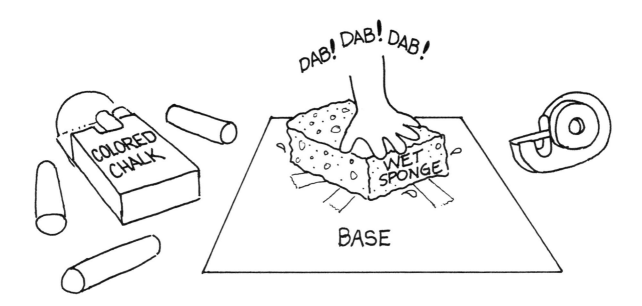

Shampoo Prints

Materials Needed:

Shampoo
Water
Electric mixer
Food coloring
Base: matte board, cardboard, or other sturdy material
Trays
Mixing bowl
Paint brushes

Procedure:

1. Pour shampoo (about 2 teaspoons) into a mixing bowl.

2. Add small amount of water and mix with electric mixer until this becomes like shaving cream.

3. Add food coloring to desired color.

4. Have child paint onto the table or tray with the mixture.

5. Lightly press base material on top of the shampoo.

Variation: Can also be used as finger paint.

Spool Printing

Materials Needed:

Different sizes of spools
Corks
Sponges
Cords or heavy yarn
Double-sided tape, or rubber cement
Paint
Shallow tray
Shallow container for paint (pie plate works well) lined with paper towel
Spoon for spreading paint
Base: matte board, cardboard, or other sturdy material

Procedure:

1. Cut the corks and sponges into various small shapes.

2. Tape these shapes onto the body of the spools. Cork, and cord or heavy yarn can be rubber cemented onto the spools.

3. Be sure that the printing material is even with the outer edge of the spools.

4. Pour a small amount of paint onto paper towel in shallow container, and spread with a spoon.

5. Let child roll the spools into the paint and then onto the base. Use various designs and create your own combination effect.

Clay Block Printing

Materials Needed:

Modeling clay
Spoon or craft sticks
Tempera
Sponges or wet rags
Paper
Shallow container for paint (pie plate works well) lined with paper towel
Spoon for spreading paint

Procedure:

1. Take a ball of modeling clay and thump it gently onto a flat surface, so that one side of the clay is flat.

2. Make a pattern or design into this flat side with a tool--craft stick or spoon handle.

3. Pour a small amount of liquid tempera onto paper towel in shallow container, and spread with a spoon.

4. Press clay design into tempera and press onto the paper. (Clay can be wiped clean with sponge or wet rag before re-using for printing.)

Plastic Clay Prints

Materials Needed:

Base: matte board, cardboard, or other sturdy material
Plasticine clay
Tile (small pieces), bangles, buttons, rings, etc.
Paint
Heavy paper
Brayer or paint brush
Block of wood, or rolling pin
Trays
Shallow container for paint (pie plate works well) lined with paper towel
Spoon for spreading paint

Procedure:

1. Give child a piece of base material and some clay.

2. Ask child to warm the clay by working with it. Child pulls small pieces of the clay off and presses them in any pattern onto the base material.

3. Let child push small tiles, buttons, bangles, etc. into the clay.

4. Paint the clay with tempera, or roll a brayer through the paint and then onto the clay so that the clay pieces have color on them.

5. Take a piece of heavy paper and press onto the clay designs. Press the back of the heavy paper with a block, or roll with a rolling pin.

6. Lift heavy paper off the clay design and see the interesting negative print.

7. Child is now free to rearrange and redesign the pattern and try again.

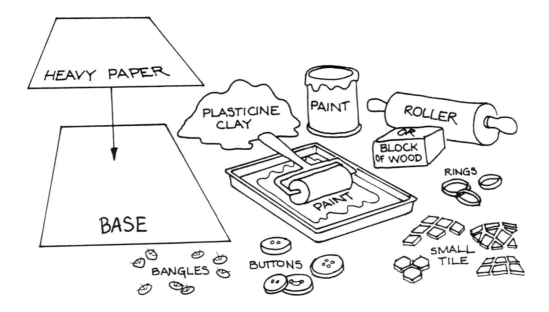

Stamp Making

Materials Needed:

Plaster of Paris
Paper or styrofoam cup
Scissors
Non-drying modeling clay
Beads, bangles, corks, buttons, tiles, etc.
Paint
Base: matte board, cardboard, or other sturdy material
Shallow container for paint (pie plate works well) lined with paper towel
Spoon for spreading paint

Procedure:

1. Cut cup about 1/2 way down from the top.

2. Put clay into the bottom of the cup.

3. Let child push various printing materials--beads, buttons, bangles, tiles, etc.--into the clay.

4. Pour plaster of Paris mixture into the cup about one inch thick.

5. Let the plaster harden and take it out of the cup. Remove clay.

6. This is the child's new self-created stamp.

7. Pour small amount of paint onto paper towel in shallow container, and spread with a spoon.

8. Press stamp into the paint and onto the base material to make a print.

Rubber Stamp Block Printing

Materials Needed:

Blocks of wood (3" x 2")
Double stick tape
Rubber bands of various sizes and widths
Paint or stamp pads
Base: matte board, cardboard, or other sturdy material
Shallow container for paint (pie plate works well) lined with paper towel
Spoon for spreading paint

Procedure:

1. Cover one entire side of the wood block with double stick tape.

2. Child can now arrange rubber bands or cut up pieces of rubber bands onto the sticky tape to create a unique stamp.

3. Pour small amount of paint onto paper towel in shallow container, and spread with a spoon.

4. Press this stamp into the paint or onto the stamp pad and then onto the base material.

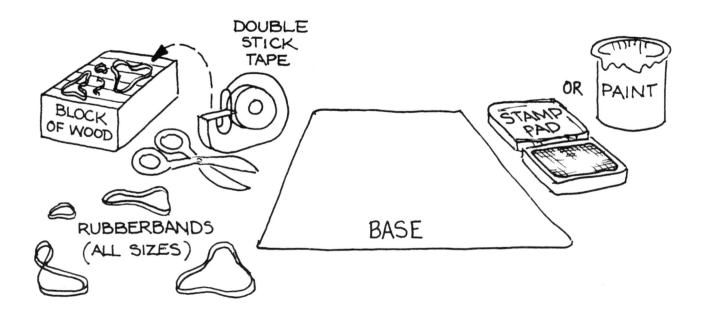

Glue Rubbing Prints

Materials Needed:

White glue in squeeze bottle
Base: matte board, cardboard, or other sturdy material
Light weight paper
Peeled crayons or chalk
Masking tape

Procedure:

1. Each child can squeeze white glue onto the base material in any design.

2. Let the glue dry overnight.

3. Tape the light weight paper over the dried glue design.

4. Rub the paper with the side of a crayon or with chalk to make a print.

5. Remove the paper and see the print. Glue boards can be re-used.

Lace Doily Prints

Materials Needed:

Variety of different sizes and shapes of doilies
Colored construction paper
White tempera paint
Trays or dishes for paint
Paint brushes or sponges

Procedure:

1. Put paint into trays or dishes.

2. Let child choose a piece of construction paper.

3. Have child arrange the doilies or doily pieces onto the construction paper.

4. Dip the brush or the sponge into the paint and lightly cover the doilies with paint. (Try to encourage child not to use too much paint because the doily will rip.)

5. After covering the doily with paint, gently lift the doilies off of the construction paper. This will give a reverse print.

Note: Some doilies can be re-used if they are not drenched.

Crumpled Foil and Paper Prints

Materials Needed:

Paint brush
Tempera paint
Base: matte board, cardboard, or other sturdy material
Aluminum foil, newspaper, brown wrapping paper
Construction paper

Procedure:

1. Paint tempera paint onto the base material, covering the board entirely. (Paint should not be too thick.)

2. Take foil, wrapping paper and/or newspaper and crumple it into a ball.

3. Now roll this crumpled ball onto the base material which is covered with paint.

4. Roll the crumpled paper onto the construction paper and see the new and interesting print.

Note: Be sure to use various kinds of paper to crumple. You may need to continue to add paint to the base material.

Plunger Prints

Materials Needed:

Large butcher paper
Cookie sheets
Liquid tempera
Plungers (yes, from the bathroom)
Tape

Procedure:

1. Roll out a large piece of butcher paper onto the floor and tape down.

2. Place a small amount of liquid tempera on the cookie sheets and place these sheets around the butcher paper.

3. Child dips the plunger into the paint and then onto the paper, thus creating a unique print.

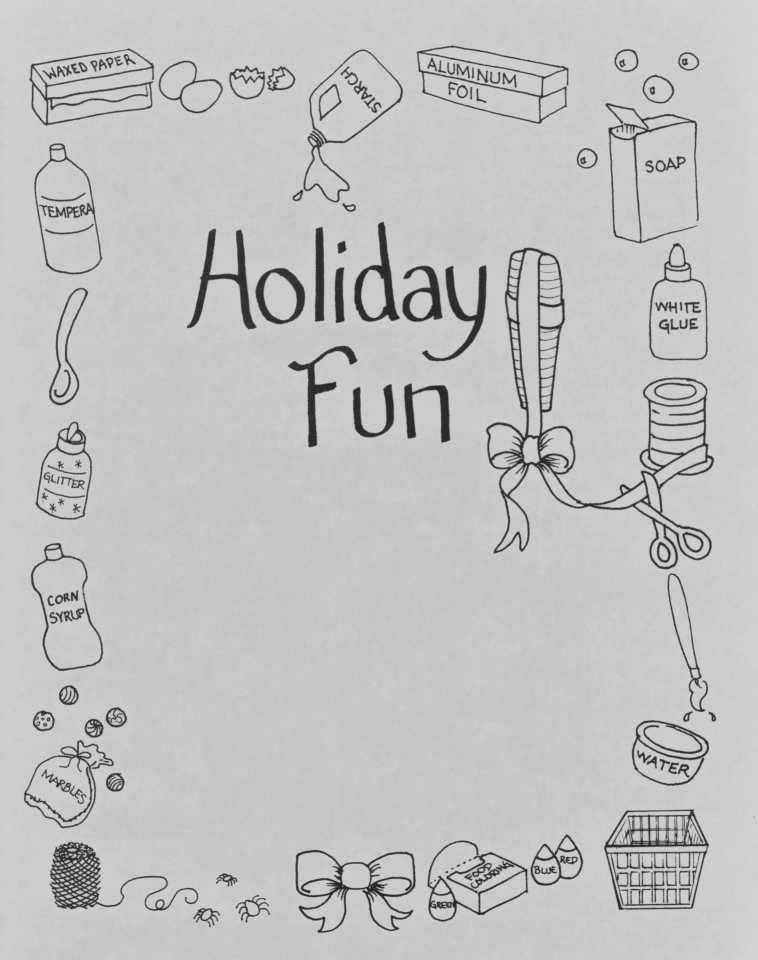

About Holiday and Theme Ideas

A word of caution concerning holiday and theme ideas. There is a risk in trying to acknowledge any holiday or theme because often the art experiences which are presented become very product-oriented rather than process-oriented.

I would encourage you to tell the parents that making holiday gifts or decorations are simply not age appropriate for preschool children and they often become a source of stress and chaos in the classroom.

Instead of trying to accommodate the parent's wishes for something cute and "holiday-ish", keep in mind that the art experiences are for the children to feel successful and free. The typical holiday treasures are often the hard work of the teachers while the children add little to the creation. Encourage your parents to welcome creative, child-oriented treasures because this is what excites the child about art.

All of the activities presented in this book and in *Dribble Drabble* can be used as holiday or theme ideas by simply cutting the base material into the appropriate theme shapes. For example, Crumpled Foil and Paper Prints creates beautiful wrapping paper for any special occasion. Doily Printing would be nice done on a heart shape for Valentine's Day. Egg yolk painting makes very glossy paint and results which would be great for Christmas, Chanukah or Easter. Snow Painting works well with a Winter Theme. Sponges cut into various shapes and used with Chalk Painting can accommodate most any theme. Be creative and inventive with holiday and themes--but stay away from product-oriented results.

I realize that there are times when it is necessary to try to find appropriate theme and holiday ideas. Following are what I would consider age appropriate, process-oriented holiday ideas.

Berry Basket Christmas Tree Ornaments

Materials Needed:

Plastic berry baskets
Cookie sheet
Aluminum foil
Glitter
Ribbon
Oven

Procedure:

1. Cover the cookie sheet with foil.

2. Put the berry basket (whole) on the foil.

3. Let child sprinkle the basket with glitter. Most of the glitter will fall in a circle under the basket--that's okay.

4. Put the whole basket and glitter into a 350° oven for two to six minutes (it takes some baskets longer to melt).

5. When the basket is completely melted, take the cookie sheet out of the oven and let it cool for about 30 seconds.

6. Remove basket from foil. Tie a ribbon onto this and hang as an ornament.

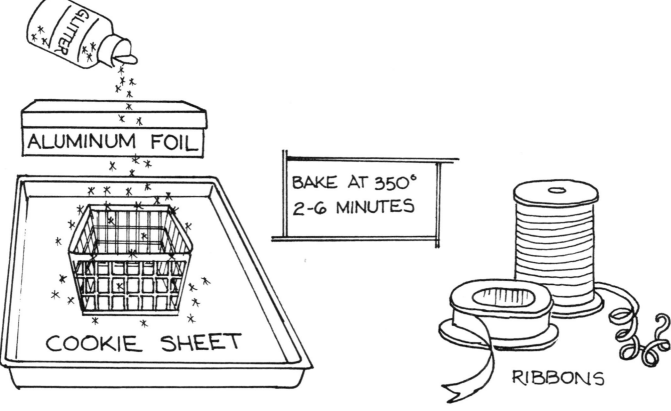

Shimmer and Shine Wrapping Paper
for All Occasions

Materials Needed:

Heavy duty aluminum foil
Tissue paper
Child-safe varnish or glue (thinned with water)
Paint brush
Containers

Procedure:

1. Tear or cut up tissue paper into small pieces.

2. Give each child a piece of foil which would be large enough to use as wrapping paper.

3. Arrange pieces of tissue onto the foil in any pattern.

4. Brush the varnish or watered down glue onto the tissue which is on the foil. Let it soak through.

Note: Possible uses for this:

Holiday wrap
Wall decoration
Greeting cards

Variation: Confetti can be sprinkled onto the glue before it dries.

Tissue Eggs

Materials Needed:

Tissue paper (cut or torn in any way by teacher and/or children)
Hard boiled eggs
Liquid starch
Paint or glue brushes
Glitter
Small containers

Procedure:

1. Put starch into small containers.

2. Let child paint starch onto the eggs.

3. Stick pieces of tissue paper to the starch. Colors will blend.

4. Sprinkle with glitter if desired.

Free Form Ornaments

Materials Needed:

String cut into various lengths
Glue (thinned with water)
Waxed paper
Glitter
Bowls for watered-down glue
Wet rag
Scissors

Procedure:

1. Let child dip the string into watered down glue and wipe excess glue off by running between the fingers. (Have a wet rag ready.)

2. Plop the string onto the waxed paper in any free form.

3. Sprinkle glitter on.

4. Let dry and peel off. Hang for an ornament.

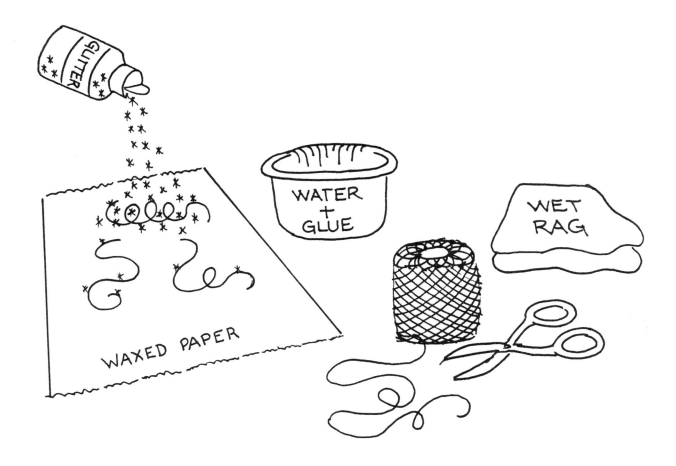

Shiny Art Painting for the Holidays

Materials Needed:

Corn syrup
Liquid tempera paint or food coloring
Liquid dishwashing or hand soap
Food coloring
Measuring spoons
Base: matte board, cardboard, or other sturdy material
Tissue paper
Small containers
Paint brush, string, or marbles
Mixing spoons

Mixture:

1 1/2 teaspoon soap
4 tablespoons corn syrup
Liquid tempera or food coloring for color

1. Mix ingredients. Stir well. Pour into small containers.

Procedure:

1. Paint with the mixture using any approach.

Note: The effect is very glossy and pretty making it appropriate for any theme or holiday.

Spider Plops

Materials Needed:

Large and small rubber/plastic spiders
Elastic string
Paint
Paper
Shallow container for paint (pie plate works well) lined with paper towel
Spoon for spreading paint

Procedure:

1. Tie elastic string onto the spider bodies.

2. Pour small amount of paint onto paper towel in shallow container, and spread with spoon.

3. Let child plop the spider into the paint, then plop onto the paper. See the spider print.

Thanksgiving Painting Ideas

Materials Needed:

Popcorn
Paper--all different shapes
Liquid tempera
Bowls for paint

Procedure:

1. Let child eat his or her fill of popcorn.

2. Now take a piece of popcorn and dip it into the paint, then onto the paper. Child can dab, rub or whatever.

3. Don't worry if the popcorn sticks to the paper.

Materials Needed:

Cornstalks
Paper
Liquid tempera
Bowls for paint

Procedure:

1. Let child choose a cornstalk.

2. Dip cornstalk into the paint and use it as a paint brush to make a design on the paper.

Note: Cornstalks were used as paint brushes in the Native American culture.

Valentine Love Box

Materials Needed:

Any size or shape of box
Wrapping paper or paint
Decoration materials--curling ribbon, glitter, stickers, metallic cord, lace, etc.
Glue or tape

Procedure:

1. Let child wrap or paint the box.

2. Decorate the box with the decorating materials.

3. This becomes the child's very special box to give as a gift to whomever it seems appropriate. The following poem can be attached if desired.

This is a very special gift, that you can never see.

The reason it's so special, is it's just to you from me.

Whenever you are lonely or even feeling blue,

You only have to hold this gift and know I think of you.

You can never unwrap it, please leave the ribbon tied.

Just hold the box close to you heart, it's filled with love inside.

Index